Sonnets on Love and Death

BY

Jean de Sponde

TRANSLATION and COMMENTARY

BY

ROBERT NUGENT

GREENWOOD PRESS, PUBLISHERS
WESTPORT, CONNECTICUT

Library of Congress Cataloging in Publication Data

Sponde, Jean de, 1557-1595.
   Sonnets on love and death.

   English and French, with commentary in English.
   Reprint of the ed. published by Lake Erie College
Press, Painesville, Ohio, which was issued as v. 2 of
Lake Erie College studies.
     1. Sonnets, French--Translations into English.
2. Sonnets, English--Translations from French.

I. Nugent, Robert. II. Title. III. Series: Lake
Erie College studies ; v. 2.
[PQ1705.S7A26 1979]   841'.3   78-12395
ISBN 0-313-21126-4

Reprinted in 1979 by Greenwood Press, Inc.,
51 Riverside Avenue, Westport, CT 06880

Printed in the United States of America

10 9 8 7 6 5 4 3 2 1

CONTENTS

Introduction

I. Sponde and the Sixteenth Century

Sponde's life is a typical one—if the typical exists in so turbulent an age as France's sixteenth century—of his time. His career and activities mirror the concerns and the achievements of the Renaissance; his thoughts and his problems represent the mood of inquiry into new studies and new beliefs emerging in that period of transition.

Scholars know more about Sponde than they do about Scève or Shakespeare. The details have been filled in by modern research, although a great deal of his biography remains conjectural. He was born in the Basque country in 1557. The family was probably Spanish in origin, austerely Calvinist in belief and practice. His education stemmed from Humanism: he early became an excellent Hellenist (his edition of Homer was later used by Chapman). He travelled to Basel and there made contacts with Humanist-Protestant activity. His interests were more than philological: he was an alchemist as well as a poet. It was a time of civil war in France; the years before his conversion (in 1593, after a period of imprisonment) were filled with various adventures. He was close to important people, the King, Henry IV, among them. After his conversion he retired to Bordeaux, where he died in 1595 and was buried in the cathedral of St. André.

Sponde's poetry is clearly a "private" production. For his contemporaries Sponde was a humanist, a translator, a jurist, a polemicist; the poems were not a part of his contemporary fame. They are the probable result—as far as present day studies can ascertain— of crises through which the poet passed: the first in the experience of love; the second— more profound and possibly more deeply felt— of religious belief. Such examination of emotions is characteristic of the age, yet critics today find that the poetry of the Pléiade, and especially of Ronsard, evinces a sense of order and harmony in the universe which foretells the classical poise of the seventeenth century.

Subsequently, certain poets and writers in the sixteenth century worked out a solution, a moral synthesis, termed Baroque, which could accept and combine life and morality in a world and a poetry dominated by images of bloodshed, of exaggerated horror, and of religious propaganda. Sponde searches, however, for spiritual or emotional equilibrium, or any combination of one with the other. His world is not an harmonious continuum of created world and its Creator nor can it reconcile opposites through balancing of tensions. If a useful word is needed to describe Sponde's position it could be called Mannerist; scholars have already defined this concept, especially in describing Bronzino and Parmegianino in the fine arts, and certain works of Carissimi and Gesualdo and some of Monteverdi in music.

II.   Sponde and Modern Poetry

Sponde remained in almost complete oblivion until recently, when he was "re-discovered" along with other poets of the late sixteenth and early seventeenth centuries. As Donne and the metaphysicals have been integrated into the modern tradition in England, so in France scholars and critics are attempting to re-define the poetic past. This attempt proceeds from the meaning and use of poetry since Baudelaire. Meaning has become less dependent upon the anecdotal and the narrative, in the manner of the Romantics. Poetry is still personal; but "personal" has come to mean what it meant for Baudelaire— the discovery of one's own notion of the beautiful. The use of poetry, consequently, is to suggest the presence of this individual search, the poem itself being the very laboratory where these esthetic investigations take place. This often mysterious, frequently anguished search is the poem in a very real way.

This kind of search is essentially modern. Valéry once wrote *Angoisse, mon véritable métier.* The basis for *angoisse* for Valéry was, of course, a choice between classical *choix*, intellect, *rigueur*, as against *hâte, abandon, firmament.* Beauty, then, for today's poet, rests on the tension between his view of the world around him and his concept of himself. Such a notion of beauty is certainly Sponde's, for his poetry expresses a similar anguish— caught between constant, unchanging values or experiences and those aspects of himself and of the world which are subject to change. For Valéry, esthetic achievement is represented by the extent to which the poet comes to an understanding of these various concerns, the realization that the poem itself is experience. For Sponde, the experience of love and death is obviously a "lived" experience. The reader has the conviction, in going through the poems, that the poet is struggling to come to an understanding of what has happened to him, and because of this struggle, he continues to experience the several dilemmas of love and death.

I think that when we read Sponde we should read him in this light, as our contemporary. Upon finishing a poem by Sponde, we feel that we have experienced what the poet himself suffered. We are more than spectators or listeners; we have become in quite a real sense participators in the struggle, in the restlessness, in the dilemmas. For the modern reader, poetry— to be meaningful and to be permanent—must have these qualities. This is probably the reason why we have discovered Sponde and have effaced the distance between ourselves and him.

III. Sponde and the Metaphysical Tradition

Recently, critics and scholars, in speaking of Sponde's poetry, have styled his verse metaphysical and have related it to Donne's in particular. Yet I think that if we speak of Donne as metaphysical, we should always bear in mind the religious system from which he derived; the poem, in Donne, proceeds— both in its development and its use of resources— from an exposition of a creed that is eternally true. Because of this belief, we find beneath the distress, beneath the progress of the poem, a tendency, ultimately, to seize movement and hold it fast. Sponde is equally distressed; the force, however, of that distress is always existential, "becoming." Such is the characteristic of his style, his choice of images, of moving earth and suns and flowing seas.

We might think of Sponde in relation to an earlier genera-
tion of writers in England than Donne's. A basic restlessness
underlies the prolixity of style and plot in Lyly and Sydney; a
cynicism, found occasionally later in Shakespeare, which leaves
the problem of love unsolved is evident in Ralegh's line *Yet what
is love, I pray thee show* ("A Description of Love"). The other
side of the Mannerist coin— the religious or idealist or spir-
itualist— could be found in the complexity of attitudes which
underlies Hooker's attempt to define doctrine, or in the selection
and rejection of elements of a past tradition which form the basis
for a unified spiritual life in Andrewes's *Preces Privatæ*. In
France, we can describe the artificiality, or early Preciosity, of
Bertaut and the emotional tensions of Malherbe's early poetry
within the boundaries of Mannerist restlessness.

Yet this kind of analysis in literary terms, or schools, should
inevitably bring the reader back to Sponde, the man and the poet.
For Sponde this underlying restlessness shows, for the most part,
an attempt to escape from a threatening chaos which could
prevail if passion were left uncontrolled, if the spiritual forces
of belief were to become disparate or scattered. Unlike an earlier
poet, Scève, who did succeed in working his way out of the de-
structive nature of overwhelming passion, Sponde is continu-
ously searching for a means of controlling the disastrous elements
of this experience. Unlike later poets, such as d'Aubigné or
Milton, Sponde achieves no all-encompassing "religious" view
of himself or of his world; even his Catholicism is tinged with
Stoicism.

IV. Love and Death in Sponde

Thus Sponde could not ignore the religious problem and
found in it, as in love, a dilemma of acceptance and refusal, to
accept this life or to seek the other. Two doctrines which deal
with these questions and which predominate in the sixteenth
century are Petrarchism and Platonism. Undoubtedly further
scholarly research will indicate how much of each is to be read
into the poems: the Petrarchan notion of the torment of love,
the idea that love is beauty leading us to the divine (a probable

influence of Platonism) and emblems such as the eyes of the beloved, are evident. Traces of Christian Neo-Platonism also appear.

I believe, however, there is a concept of love in Sponde which is truly his because the experience is truly his. He treats love as a personal interrogation— its reasons, its origins, its inevitability— and thus shows his basic distress. This seeking of love is carried out as a kind of necessity— keenly and personally felt— of the experience of love. The experience is more than imagined: it can be considered as a part of the physical world. Throughout the poems on love, Sponde's notion of reality is deeply physical. Although his preoccupation is to understand the physical properties of the world, he could never state firmly and without hesitation that the universe was steady, immutable. He is continually preoccupied with constancy—physical, almost chemical in its significance, but he also desires to come to an understanding of mutability—whether of planets that move or stars that change their positions; this dichotomy allows him no rest.

Sponde's inner world resembles his outer world: in neither is a final solution completely acceptable or accepted. One wonders, then, about his conversion. Was this the final way, the ultimate repose? The religious poetry is not autobiographical. Sponde does not tell us what happened that would lead him to this step, what possible disappointment in his worldly affairs or what death of friend or loved one. But the reader is sure of one thing— the sense of the powerful personal emotion he receives in reading the poems.

As with other poets to whom today we give the name "pure" (Mallarmé, for example), we are aware of the poet only in view of the poetry he writes. Sponde takes a common theme of the century, man coming to terms with death, with his own death; yet this experience is set forth with so profound a conviction, it is so refined in a chemical sense, that we study the poems as pure experience. The note of this anguish is so personal that we come closer to him than we could to a poet about whom, or to a poem about which, we knew everything.

Translator's Note

I have modernized the spelling of the French wherever changes do not interfere with rhyme or meter. The translations are meant to be a little more than literal, yet without obtruding the editor's own personality onto one forceful enough to stand by itself.

The brief comments are designed as possible readings of the poems from which the individual student can proceed on his own.

The text used is that established by François Ruchon and Alan Boase in their edition published in *Les Trésors de la littérature française* (Genève, 1949).

Five of the translations appear in an anthology of translations of Renaissance poetry edited by H. M. Priest for Northwestern University Press.

SONNETS

on
LOVE
and
DEATH

Sonnets d'amour

I

Si c'est dessus les eaux que la terre est pressée,
Comment se soutient-elle encor si fermement?
Et si c'est sur les vents qu'elle a son fondement,
Qui la peut conserver sans être renversée?

Ces justes contrepoids qui nous l'ont balancée,
Ne penchent-ils jamais d'un divers branlement?
Et qui nous fait solide ainsi cet Elément,
Qui trouve autour de lui l'inconstance amassée?

Il est ainsi: ce corps se va tout soulevant
Sans jamais s'ébranler parmi l'onde et le vent.
Miracle nonpareil! si mon amour extrême,

Voyant ces maux coulants, soufflants de tous cotés,
Ne trouvait tous les jours par exemple de même
Sa constance au milieu de ces légèretés.

If the earth is pressed down by the seas
Which lie about it, how does the earth so firmly hold?
And if it is upon the winds that the world's foundation lies,
What prevents it from being overturned?
These lawful counterweights which kept the balance
Of the world for us, do they not ever yield upon an outside force?
And what makes this element so steady,
Which finds itself surrounded by threats of instability?
This is why: this body continues to bear all
Without ever breaking amidst the wave or wind.
Unparalleled miracle! if my highest love,
On seeing these evils ebb and flow on every side,
Were not to find therein a like example
Of its own constancy amid changing nature's will.

Sponde declares his doctrine of love in the first sonnet. This preoccupation is continually expressed in physical terms in the sense of a concern over physical balance, balance of physical forces. The earth resists the pressure of the ocean and the up-setting power of the wind. Thus the body, by its inner force, bears up against change. The compulsion of love is the power to resist inconstancy. The corresponding balance is expressed as *extrême*, the furthermost limit of emotional tension, which resolves the question posed by the two contradictory directions, constancy and change.

Sonnets d'amour

II

Quand je vois les efforts de ce grand Alexandre,
D'un César dont le sein comblé de passions
Embrase tout du feu de ses ambitions,
Et n'en laisse après soi mémoire qu'en la cendre :

Quand je vois que leur gloire est seulement de rendre
(Après l'orage enflé de tant d'afflictions)
Calmes dessous leurs lois toutes les nations
Qui voient le Soleil et monter et descendre :

Encor que j'ai de quoi m'enorgueillir comme eux,
Que mes lauriers ne soient de leurs lauriers honteux,
Je les condamne tous et ne les puis défendre :

Ma belle, c'est vers toi que tournent mes esprits,
Ces tyrans-là faisaient leur triomphe de prendre,
Et je triompherai de ce que tu m'as pris.

When I see the efforts of this great Alexander,

Of a Cæsar whose breast filled with passions

Sets all ablaze with his ambitions' fire

And after him leaves remembrance of them but in the ashes:

When I see that their fame is only to render

(After the storm swollen with so many afflictions)

Calm beneath their laws all nations

Which see the sun both rise and set:

Although I have reason to pride myself as they,

That my laurels might not of their laurels unworthy be,

I condemn them all and in their defense I cannot stand.

My love, my mind turns towards you: those tyrants

Took their triumph in what they captured,

And I shall triumph from that which you stole from me.

Sponde's preoccupation has to do with the unending nature of love. He takes his example from history, with emphasis upon the contrast established between *feu et cendre, orage* and *calmes.* The rising and setting sun makes the contrast one of universal or lasting truth. But his love has a universal aspect, too; his mind turns towards the beloved, who has seized his passion. Unlike the tyrant's fame, which has turned to ashes, the poet will achieve immortality through love. There is the Mannerist paradox: one fire, which has overcome this world, has become ashes, a kind of annihilation; another, the flame of love, deprived, remains *feu,* its own true nature.

Sonnets d'amour

III

Qui serait dans les cieux, et baisserait sa vue
Sur le large pourpis de ce sec élément
Il ne croirait le Tout rien qu'un point seulement,
Un point encor caché du voile d'une nue :

Mais s'il contemple après cette courtine bleue,
Ce cercle de cristal, ce doré firmament,
Il juge que son tour est grand infiniment,
Et que cette grandeur nous est toute inconnue.

Ainsi de ce grand ciel, ou l'amour m'a guidé,
De ce grand ciel d'Amour où mon oeil est bandé,
Si je relâche un peu la pointe aiguë au reste,

Au reste des amours, je vois sous une nuit
Le monde d'Epicure en atomes réduit,
Leur amour tout de terre, et le mien tout céleste.

Whoever were to stand in the heavens, and lower then his sight

Upon the wide display of this dry element,

He would believe all this to be only a single

Mark, a mark still hidden by a cloudy veil:

But if he contemplate, from here, beyond that blue curtain,

That crystal circle, that golden firmament,

He would judge that his eyes' voyage across the skies is
*   infinitely vast*

And that such grandeur is, to us, totally unknown.

Thus of this great heaven, where love has guided me so sure,

Of this great heaven of love o'er which my eye is stretched:

If I unbend a little my keen attention to the other,

To the other loves, I see under a night's pall

The world of Epicurus, to atoms now reduced:

Their love all of earth, and mine celestial.

The notion of perspective here is similar to the distortion found in Mannerist paintings. The viewpoint is first from above, looking at *le Tout,* which seems its opposite, *rien.* The eye travels upwards through materials (cloth, crystal, gold), which have a kind of transparency, yet which hide the infinite vast spaces. The two lines of view do not meet except insofar as the poet shifts (from his celestial vantage point) to regard the world of inconstant love, lost in the confusion of Epicurean atoms. It would seem that Sponde desires unity, oneness: his attempt is "interposed," indicating an inability to achieve either a Classical or Baroque poise.

Sonnets d'amour

IV

En vain mille beautés à mes yeux se présentent,
Mes yeux leur sont ouverts et mon courage clos,
Une seule beauté s'enflamme dans mes os
Et mes os de ce feu seulement se contentent :

Les rigueurs de ma vie et du temps, qui m'absentent
Du bien-heureux séjour où loge mon repos,
Altèrent moins mon âme, encor que mon propos
Et mes discrets désirs jamais ne se repentent.

Chatouilleuses beautés, vous domptez doucement
Tous ces esprits flottants, qui souillent aisément
Des absentes amours la chaste souvenance :

Mais pour tous vos efforts je demeure indompté :
Ainsi je veux servir d'un patron de constance,
Comme ma belle fleur d'un patron de beauté.

In vain a thousand beauties tempt my eyes,

My eyes are open to them and my courage closed,

A single beauty takes fire in my bones

And my bones with this fire only satisfied:

The hardships of my life and of time, which absent

Me from that most happy place where dwells all my repose,

Change less my soul than does their beauty, though my intention

And my secret desires will never seek repentance's ruse.

Frivolous beauties, you sweetly tame

All wavering spirits, those who easily stain

The chaste remembrance of distant love's delight:

But despite all your efforts, I yet remain the same:

Thus I should serve as a model for constant pain,

As does my pretty flower a model for beauty's sight.

———————

The poem states that the eyes of the court beauties have less effect than do the hardships imposed by circumstances. The tone is one of conceits: the poet's eyes are full of the beauty of this world (yet he will not cede to it and abandon his distant love); his bones are filled with the flame of love (yet this love is physically absent). Beneath this tone, however, we discover—once more—Sponde's sincerity. We read in the poem an insistence on his need for a single experience of love in the face of the diffuseness and the general shifting, changing nature of life. Sponde's quest is repeated again and again throughout the poems.

Sonnets d'amour

V

Je meurs, et les soucis qui sortent du martyre
Que me donne l'absence, et les jours et les nuits
Font tant qu'à tous moments je ne sais que je suis,
Si j'empire du tout ou bien si je respire.

Un chagrin survenant mille chagrins m'attire,
Et me cuidant aider moi-même je me nuis;
L'infini mouvement de mes roulants ennuis
M'emporte, et je le sens, mais je ne le puis dire.

Je suis cet Actéon de ses chiens déchiré!
Et l'éclat de mon âme est si bien altéré
Qu'elle, qui devrait me faire vivre, me tue:

Deux Déesses nous ont tramé tout notre sort,
Mais pour divers sujets nous trouvons même mort,
Moi de ne la voir point, et lui de l'avoir vue.

I die: the worries which emerge from the martyrdom

Your absence gives me, leave me in such torture

Both day and night, that at each moment I know not if I am

Alive, whether from all this more ill, or even if I breathe.

A misfortune occurs and draws in its wake a thousand more;

And in thinking that I might cure myself, I do myself harm.

The infinite movement of each changing care

Takes hold of me and I feel it to be so, but I cannot give it name.

I am that Actæon torn by his dogs!

And the brightness of my soul has become so obscure

That she who should make live, kills.

Two goddesses have woven for us our lives' course.

But for different reasons we find the same death:

I in not seeing my love at all, he for having seen his love's smile.

The terrible struggle in Sponde's mind to come to terms with absence, doubts, questions, involved in the experience of love, is stylistically reflected in sounds (the repetition of the consonants *m* and *n*, for example), in the running over of lines (*martyre que me donne l'absence*). The theme underlying this agitation is basically love and death, presence and absence, good and evil. But there is no resolution, neither in his mind nor in his body; nor is it possible to project one through space (*infini*) to a future possibility. The moral obligation is not met by the woman (*elle...devrait*). The dilemma between seeing (and the destroying passion which is the result of the encounter) and not seeing (with the inevitable pangs of regret) is—for Sponde —not capable of a resolution.

Sonnets d'amour

VI

Mon Dieu, que je voudrais que ma main fût oisive,
Que ma bouche et mes yeux reprissent leur devoir!
Ecrire est peu: c'est plus de parler et de voir,
De ces deux oeuvres l'une est morte et l'autre vive.

Quelque beau trait d'amour que notre main écrive,
Ce sont témoins muets qui n'ont pas le pouvoir
Ni le semblable poids, que l'oeil pourrait avoir
Et de nos vives voix la vertu plus naïve.

Mais quoi? n'étaient encor ces faibles étançons
Et ces fruits mi-rongés dont nous le nourrissons
L'Amour mourrait de faim et cherrait en ruine:

Ecrivons, attendant de plus fermes plaisirs,
Et si le temps domine encor sur nos désirs,
Faisons que sur le temps la constance domine.

My God, how I would wish my hand were slower,

That my mouth and eyes should take up again their duty!

To write is little: it is worth more to speak and see:

Of these two works one is dead, the other live.

However fine a story of love our hand might write,

Words are but mute witness and have not the power

Nor the necessary weight that the weakest strength

Of living voice could have.

Ah then! Were it not for these feeble props

*And these half-gnawed fruits with which we nourish its **ardor**,*

Love would die of hunger and fall into ruins.

Let us write, while waiting for surer pleasures.

And if time still holds sway over desires,

Let us act so that constancy holds sway over time's hour.

———————

On one level Sponde proposes the statement, frequently asserted by Renaissance poets, of immortality through poetry. On a deeper level, it is Sponde speaking directly to us; we are reminded of Baudelaire's *ton de confessionnal*. The writing of verse can not make up for love; nor, more intensely, is the insufficiency of verse to be disregarded. It is—too often—all that we have to keep love from disintegrating. The poet through poetry overcomes time's inconstancy and yet does not withstand its destruction: a similar parallel is established in the emotional sphere.

Sonnets d'amour

VII

Si j'avais comme vous, mignardes colombelles,
Des plumages si beaux sur mon corps attachés,
On aurait beau tenir mes esprits empêchés
De l'indomptable fer de cent châines nouvelles:

Sur les ailes du vent je guiderais mes ailes,
J'irais jusqu'au séjour où mes biens sont cachés:
Ainsi voyant de moi ces ennuis arrachés,
Je ne sentirais plus ces absences cruelles.

Colombelles hélas! que j'ai bien souhaité
Que mon corps vous semblât autant d'agilité
Que mon âme d'amour à votre âme ressemble!

Mais quoi? je le souhaite et me trompe d'autant.
Ferais-je bien voler un amour si constant
D'un monde tout rempli de vos ailes ensemble?

If I like you, sweet doves, had, fastened

To my body, such fine feathers,

In vain would my wits be constrained

By the firm iron of a hundred new chains.

Upon the wings of the wind I would guide my wings,

I would go to the dwelling place of my fortune's hidden good;

Thus, on seeing this distress torn from my mind,

I would no longer feel these cruel absences.

Doves, alas! How truly I have wished

That my body might resemble yours in agile

Flight, and—as much—my soul of love your soul!

And then? I wish it so and am mistaken accordingly.

Would I do well to rob a love which loves so constantly,

From a world with your wings all filled?

The theme of this sonnet is wings: the wings of the dove, the wind, and soul. The implication is neo-Platonic; the desire to flee to the ideal, the search for the desired *séjour*. It forecasts Mallarmé's *pureté* and *azur*. Yet this achievement is impossible (*on aurait beau tenir*): he must remain close to the *amour si constant*. At least, he always reminds himself that it is the *idéal* to be wished for and—once found—held. The movement of the poem is centrifugal: from dispersion, open action across space (*je guiderais mes ailes*) to enclosure, density (*vos ailes ensemble*). From this inevitability Sponde cannot escape. Romantic *évasion* and Baudelaire's *n'importe où hors de ce monde* are not yet available to poetry.

Sonnets d'amour

VIII

Ce trésor que j'ai pris avec tant de peine
Je le veux avec peine encore conserver
Tardif à reposer, prompt à me relever,
Et tant veiller qu'en fin on ne me le surprenne.

Encor que de mes yeux la garde plus certaine
Auprès de son séjour ne se puisse trouver,
Et qu'il me peut encor en l'absence arriver
Qu'un autre plus prochain me l'empoigne et l'emmène.

Je ne veux pas pourtant me travailler ainsi,
Ta seule foi m'assure et m'ôte le souci:
Et ne changera point pourvu que je ne change.

Il faut tenir bon oeil et bon pied sur ce point:
A gagner un beau bien on gagne une louange.
Mais on en gagne mille à ne le perdre point.

This treasure, which cost me so much pain to seize,
I wish to keep even now with pains:
Slow to take my rest, early to rise,
And be so much awake that no one ever steal it from me.
Although my eyes' most certain custody
Next to this treasure's dwelling place may not be found,
And that—while absent—it can still happen to me
That another, closer, might grasp it and bear it off;
Yet I do not wish to torture thus myself.
Your faith alone assures me and takes away my worry:
It will not change provided that I have not changed.
But one must be aware and on watch in this regard:
In gaining a thing of worth he gains a word of praise,
But gains a thousand if he loses not his pain's reward.

———————

Again we are convinced of the fact that, beneath the Mannerist dexterity in handling conceits, there is a real experience that assures us of the author's sincerity. The lover's attitude is, first, watchfulness. Then comes the shift to trust and confidence, based upon the notion of the reciprocal loss of love through mistrust. The two opposing forces become equal. The poet finally returns to the belief that the *trésor* is his *bien*. He concludes that the keeping of love (through either being constantly on his guard or through trust), is worth more than the initial wooing (*pris avec tant de peine*).

Sonnets d'amour

IX

Si tant de maux passés ne m'ont acquis ce bien,
Que vous croyez au moins que je vous suis fidèle,
Ou si vous le croyez, qu'à la moindre querelle
Vous me fassiez semblant de n'en plus croire rien,

Belle, pour qui je meurs, belle, pensez-vous bien
Que je ne sente point cette injure cruelle?
Plus sanglante beaucoup que la peine éternelle,
Où malgré tout le monde encor je me retiens.

Il est vrai toutefois, vos beautés infinies,
Quand je vivrais encor cent mille et mille vies,
Ne se pourraient jamais servir si dignement

Que je ne fusse en reste à leur valeur parfaite:
Mais croyez-le ou non, la preuve est toute faite
Qu'au prix de moi, l'Amour aime imparfaitement.

If these many misfortunes have gained for me this good fortune,

That you believe, at least, that I am faithful to you,

Or if you so take stock, that upon the least provocation

You might pretend to give no further trust,

Belle, *for whom I die,* belle, *do you really think*

That I do not feel at all this cruel slander?

Much more painful than eternal damnation,

In fear of which, despite all others, I still hold back.

It is true, however, that the infinite range of your beauty,

Even if I were to live a hundred thousand and yet
a thousand lives,

Could never be served so worthily

That I would not be imperfect to their perfect value:

But believe it or not, the proof is quite clear

That, compared to me, Love loves imperfectly.

The problem of love and pain is central to Sponde, which makes us think that the sonnets tell of a real experience. It concerns the basic quandary of love, fidelity. A misfortune occurs: on whom lies the responsibility and for how long does love suffer love's defeats? *La peine éternelle,* which has bothered some critics, is theologically hell, to which one is committed for acts done and undone. In a like manner, there is in love a *peine éternelle* which is easier to bear—being intellectualized—than the emotional pain of love, which Sponde's reason cannot understand, being tempered by the mocking voice of *tout le monde* to desist from faithfulness. Finally, the poet must admit that for others love is only imperfect; for himself, despite the irrationality of the experience, love is perfect.

Sonnets d'amour

X

Je ne bouge non plus qu'un écueil dedans l'onde
Qui fait fort à l'orage et le fait reculer.
Il me trouve affermi, qui cherche à m'ébranler,
Dussé-je voir branler contre moi tout le monde.

Chacun qui voit combien tous les jours je me fonde
Sur ce constant dessein, se mêle d'en parler,
Trouble la terre et l'air afin de me troubler,
Et ne pouvant rien plus, pour le moins il en gronde.

Mais je n'écoute point (que pour le mépriser)
Ce propos enchanteur qui tend à m'abuser
Et me ravir le bien que leur rage m'envie.

Laissons, laissons-les dire, un seul mot me suffit:
Qu'en la guerre d'amour une âme bien nourrie
Emporte tout l'honneur emportant le profit.

I move no more than a reef in the wave of the sea

Which withstands the storm and makes it withdraw.

Whoever seeks to overthrow me, finds me with new strength,

Even though I were to see the world take arms against me.

Each one who sees to what extent each day I place

My purpose on this unchanging plan hastens to speak thereof,

Stirs up earth and air that I may be distraught.

And, not being able to do more, complains of it,
*   since he cannot do less.*

But I do not listen to the delight

Of this proposal, except to despise it: it would hurt

Me and take from me the good that their unreason envies me.

Let us, then, let us allow them to speak: for me a single word

Suffices: in the war of love, a soul well-formed

Carries off all the honor while carrying off the profit.

———

The theme of the sonnet is, in a way, that of the war of love, with the victor carrying off the spoils. But Sponde moves his viewpoint and lowers the tone. The perspective is not a direct one between lover and beloved, the tone is less "epic" than "*précieux*." His own troubled state is reflected in the hesitation implied in the imperfect subjunctive (*dussé*), in the unchanging purpose of the verb *je me fonde*, in his refusal to participate in the world's judgements. The world in turn is one of violence (*ébranler*), of distress (*troubler*), of storm. The tone of the final resolution between the two is left unresolved, morally. At the end we are again on a somewhat ironic level.

21

Sonnets d'amour

XI

Tous mes propos jadis ne vous faisaient instance
Que de l'ardent amour dont j'étais embrasé:
Mais depuis que votre oeil sur moi s'est apaisé
Je ne puis vous parler rien que de ma constance.

L'Amour même de qui j'éprouve l'assistance,
Qui sait combien l'esprit de l'homme est fort aisé
D'aller aux changements, se tient comme abusé
Voyant qu'en vous aimant j'aime sans repentance.

Il s'en remontre assez qui brûlent vivement,
Mais la fin de leur feu, qui se va consommant,
N'est qu'un brin de fumée et qu'un morceau de cendre.

Je laisse ces amants croupir en leurs humeurs
Et me tiens pour content, s'il vous plaît de comprendre
Que mon feu ne saurait mourir si je ne meurs.

Formerly all my adoring words to you were but a show

Of my burning love with which I was on fire:

But since your eyes have smiled on me with favor,

I can speak to you only of my constant vow.

Love itself, whose help I need,

Knows how much the mind of man is predisposed

To seek out change and consider itself treated with insolence,

On seeing that in loving you I love without repentance.

Many there are who burn brightly with love.

But their fire, which keeps on consuming itself, ends

In a thread of smoke and a flake of ash.

I let these lovers stagnate in their moods

And think myself content, if it pleases you to believe

That—unless I do—my fire would not be capable of death.

Sponde's central concern is constancy, balance. He treats this theme sometimes cosmologically, at other times intellectually, starting with his own introspective dialogue on the permanence of love. The intellectualism (*propos*) is tied up with an image of immobility, his being on fire with a burning fire that cannot escape, that is in a sense imprisoned; nor when the flames die down is there any other need than constancy. The mind of man is change; the poet's love—through his mind—is constancy. The fire of others ends in another kind of immobility—smoke and ash. His fire keeps on, but it is not everlasting: it can end if the poet dies. Again resolution of an emotional problem is not fully reached.

23

Sonnets d'amour

XII

Mon coeur, ne te rends point à ces ennuis d'absence,
Et quelque forts qu'ils soient, sois encore plus fort;
Quand même tu serais sur le point de la mort,
Mon coeur, ne te rends point et reprends ta puissance.

Que si tant de combats te donnent connaissance
Que tu n'es pas toujours pour rompre leur effort,
Garde-toi de tomber dans un tel déconfort
Que ton amour jamais y perde son essence.

Puis que tous tes soupirs sont ainsi retardés,
Laisse, laisse courir ces torrents débordés,
Et monte sur les rocs de ce mont de constance:

Ainsi dessus les monts ce sage chef Romain
Différa ses combats du jour au lendemain,
Se moqua d'Hannibal, rompant sa violence.

My heart, do not surrender to these pains of absence,

And however strong they are, be yet stronger still.

Though you were on the point of death, my heart,

Do not surrender, but set out once more your own defense.

Since so many struggles give you the knowledge and the insight

That you are not always able to break their will,

Keep yourself from falling into such defeat

Lest your love ever lose therein its essence.

Since all your sighs you thus detain,

Let, O let, these flooded torrents run:

And climb, my heart, upon the rocky mount of faithfulness.

Thus upon the mountains that wise Roman leader

Put off his battles from one day to the other,

Defying Hannibal and breaking thus his force.

In the architecture, or ordering of the sonnets as a sequence, Sponde now introduces a group of poems in which an historical event or hero acts as an emblem for his mind. In this poem he gives the meaning first (in the other poems of this group the emblem precedes, the significance comes after) ; he refers to Quintus Fabius Maximus, the Cunctator ("delayer"), who maneuvered among the hills, rendering Hannibal's cavalry useless, and refused to give him battle. Thus Sponde addresses his heart, in a military fashion, as though in tactics similar to Fabius's, refusing to battle with the forces of inconstancy, going into the hills of solitude, and waiting there until these forces be exhausted. We can read an autobiographical reference here: almost as though after the struggle of the first sonnets, a moment of recollection were available upon the initial defeat of love (or an equivocal victory).

25

Sonnets d'amour

XIII

Tu disais, Archimède, ainsi qu'on nous rapporte,
Qu'on te donnât un point pour bien te soutenir,
Tu branlerais le monde, et le ferais venir,
Comme un faix plus léger de lieu en lieu s'emporte.

Puis que ton arc si beau, ta main était si forte,
Si tu pouvais encor au monde revenir,
Dans l'amour que mon coeur s'efforce à retenir
Tu trouverais ton point peut être en quelque sorte.

Pourrait-on voir jamais plus de solidité
Qu'en ce qui branle moins plus il est agité
Et prend son assurance en l'inconstance même:

Il est sûr, Archimède, et je n'en doute point:
Pour branler tout le Monde et s'assurer d'un point,
Il te fallait aimer aussi ferme que j'aime.

You used to say, Archimedes, according to what we're told,

That if you were given a point on which to stand

Firmly, you would shake the world and make it turn

As though it were a lighter burden carried from place to place.

Since your hand was so strong, your arch so fair,

If you were able to come back into the world again,

In the love that my heart strives to maintain

You would find that your point would be, in some way, there.

Could one ever see more firmness

Than in that which trembles the less the more it is moved,

And finds from inconstancy itself its assurance.

It is certain, Archimedes, and I am not the least in doubt,

That to move the whole world and to secure for yourself
        such a point,

You had to love steadfastly as I have loved.

———————

Sponde's preoccupation with physical constancy as an apology
or explanation for his emotional distress is again evident. He
takes those inventions of Archimedes which have to do with
weights and movements of weights (pivots and engines of war),
and sees in them an analogy of the weight of his own love. His
"inner world" is no less controlled by physical law than is the
"external world." His love is the pivot from which the poet
can move the world; inversely, it is also that physical property
which the more it is moved, the stronger it remains.

Sonnets d'amour

XIV

Quand le vaillant Hector, le grand rempart de Troie,
Sortit tout enflammé, sur les nefs des Grégeois,
Et qu'Achille charmait d'une plaintive voix
Son oisive douleur, sa vengeance de joie ;

Comme quand le Soleil dedans l'onde flamboie,
L'onde des rais tremblants repousse dans les toits ;
La Grèce tout ainsi flottante cette fois
Eût peur d'être à la fin la proie de sa proie.

Un seul bouclier d'Ajax se trouvant le plus fort
Soutint cette fureur et dompta cet effort.
J'eusse perdu de même en cette horrible absence.

Mon amour, assailli d'une armée d'ennuis,
Dans le travail des jours, dans la langueur des nuits ;
Si je ne l'eusse armé d'un bouclier de constance.

When valiant Hector, the great wall of Troy,

Came out all ablaze with anger upon the Grecian ships:

When Achilles sang in plaintive voice

His inaction's cause, with grief—his vengeance, with joy;

As when the Sun, within the waves, shines

And the waves send back trembling rays upon the roofs;

Greece, thus, at this time, afloat, at sea,

Would fear at last to be the prey of its own prey.

A single shield of Ajax, being the stronger,

Held up this fury and tamed this effort.

So would I have lost my love, in the terror

Of its absence: besieged by an army of doubts,

In the travail of our days, in the languor of our nights,

Had I not armed myself with constancy as my shield and armor.

The emblem is extended from the first to the tenth line: the wrath of the Trojans, the rage of war, the image of the Greek fleet with the movement of the sunlight from water to roofs (possibly of houses or of some covering over the ships' decks), the emotional perplexity and bewilderment of the Greeks, Ajax' valor. The stylistic device is the use of the emblem to describe (or stand for) the poet's feelings: the poet is in the center, protected by his shield of faithful love, surrounded all round by warfare.

Sonnets d'amour

XV

Cette brave Carthage, un des honneurs du monde
Et la longue terreur de l'empire Romain,
Qui donna tant de peine à son coeur, à sa main,
Pour se faire première, et Rome la seconde:

Après avoir dompté presque la terre et l'onde,
Et porté dans le ciel tout l'orgueil de son sein,
Eprouva mais trop tard, qu'un superbe dessein
Fondé dessus le vent, il faut en fin qu'il fonde.

Cette insolente-là! la pompe qu'elle aima!
Le brasier dévorant du feu la consuma:
Que je me ris au lieu, Carthage, de te plaindre.

Ton feu dura vingt jours, et brûla pour si peu.
Hélas! que dirais-tu si tu voyais qu'un feu
Me brûle si longtemps sans qu'il se puisse éteindre?

This brave Carthage, one of the honors of the world,

And for long the dread of the Roman Empire,

Which grieved its heart so much and wore out its hand

To make itself first and Rome second:

After nearly subduing both the earth and the seas

And raising up to heaven all the pride of its breast,

Experienced, alas, too late, that a proud purpose

Founded on wind must, at last, be dissolved.

That insolent one! the pomp that it loved!

The furnace that devours fire destroyed it.

Let me mock you, Carthage, pity you I will not.

Your fire raged twenty days, and burned for so little cause.

Alas! what would you say if you saw that a fire

Has been burning me for so long a time, a fire that can
    not be put out?

Sponde here poses the problem of the ethics of love: the Renaissance concern with pride—civic and national pride, individual
ambition. The poem can be read as a successful "imitation" of
the ancients—contained in one of the most often used images of
pride and fall, the presumption of Carthage and its destruction.
Sponde, too, has a similar *dessein superbe* of conquest. The city
was destroyed by fire; the fire of love can not be so easily
quenched. The end of love is left unanswered, unlike the *dénoue-
ment* in the tragedies of the classical Racine, where each aspect
of the love relationship involved is made clear.

Sonnets d'amour

XVI

Je prends exemple en toi, courageuse Numance,
L'un des grands fléaux de Rome, et comme toi je veux,
Pratiquant la valeur, apprendre à nos neveux
Qu'il faut vaincre en l'assaut, mourir en la défense.

Durant tes quatorze ans, l'insolente arrogance
De tes longs ennemis, du bon heur dépourvus,
Contre tant de vertu s'arrachait les cheveux
Et s'arrachait plus fort encore l'espérance :

Enfin on n'eut moyen propre à te surmonter
Que te laisser toi-même à toi-même dompter,
Et toi tu ne laissas que tes murs et ta cendre :

Ainsi tous ces ennuis dont je vaincs les efforts,
S'ils se trouvent enfin plus rusés que plus forts,
J'aime mieux comme toi mourir que de me rendre.

I take my example from you, courageous Numantia,

One of the great scourges of Rome; like you, through the practice

Of valor, I want to teach our posterity the lesson

That one must conquer in the assault, die in the defense.

For fourteen years you endured the insolent arrogance

Of your fixed enemies, who, deprived of success,

Against so much courage tore out their hair,

And even more did they of hope despair.

Finally, there was no more suitable manner

To overcome you than to let yourself tame yourself:

And you, you left nothing but your walls and ashes

Thus all afflictions' forces that I vanquish,

If—at the end—they are more cunning than powerful,

Like you, I prefer to die than to surrender.

Numantia fought against Rome, which wasted in that struggle *vertu* (courage) and *espérance* (hope). Numantia finally gave in after a siege, reduced by hunger, a victory to be celebrated in Roman history along with the defeat of Carthage. The analogy is clearly drawn: in the warfare of love, the poet would accept victory only through courage and patience. Rather than win love through stratagem, the poet prefers to die. The somewhat commonplace nature of the comparison is relieved by Sponde's sincerity. We are convinced that the choice, *mourir, me rendre*, is heartfelt, *vécu*; the choice also implies more than a kind of *amour courtois*, an attitude of religious or philosophical inquiry underlying the sequence as a whole.

Sonnets d'amour

XVII

Je sens dedans mon âme une guerre civile,
D'un parti ma raison, mes sens d'autre parti,
Dont le brûlant discord ne peut être amorti,
Tant chacun son tranchant l'un contre l'autre affile.

Mais mes sens sont armés d'un verre si fragile
Que si le coeur bientôt ne s'en est départi,
Tout l'heur vers ma raison se verra converti,
Comme au parti plus fort, plus juste et plus utile.

Mes sens veulent ployer sous ce pesant fardeau
Des ardeurs que me donne un éloigné flambeau;
Au rebours, la raison me renforce au martyre.

Faisons comme dans Rome, à ce peuple mutin
De mes sens inconstants, arrachons-les enfin!
Et que notre raison y plante son Empire.

I feel within my soul a civil war:

On the one side, my reason, on the other, my senses stand.

Their burning discord can not be deadened,

So much the cutting edge of one is sharpened against the other.

But my senses are armed with a glass-like fragility

So that my heart is not soon broken by this discord;

All fortune's outcome will be converted to my reason,

As though to the strongest, most just, and most useful side.

My senses would bend under this heavy burden

Of the ardors that a distant torch gives to me:

Against my will, reason strengthens me for a martyr's fate.

Let us deal, as in Rome, with the unruly mob

Of my wavering senses: at last, let us tear them out!

And let our reason plant herein its domain.

The discord and disparity between the senses and the reason are likened to civil war, which for Sponde—as for Montaigne—was the most dreadful form of war. Both writers felt the need of harmony in the civil state and a similar harmony in one's emotional and physical state. Yet Sponde never reached Montaigne's conclusion; Sponde could believe that reason seems by far the more powerful force and inflicts the sharpest pain, and that the senses should be done away with if they can not bear the pangs of distant love. The verb *plante* makes us think of the fourth spleen poem of Baudelaire. But whereas in Baudelaire the poem delves progressively deeper into horror, Sponde's sonnet wavers (as do the fortunes of war) ; we wonder whether the final commitment to reason is forever viable.

Sonnets d'amour

XVIII

Ne vous étonnez point si mon esprit, qui passe
De travail en travail par tant de mouvements,
Depuis qu'il est banni dans ces éloignements,
Tout agile qu'il est, ne change point de place.

Ce que vous en voyez, quelque chose qu'il fasse,
Il s'est planté si bien sur si bons fondements,
Qu'il ne voudrait jamais souffrir de changements,
Si ce n'est que le feu se peut changer de place.

Ces deux contraires sont en moi seul arrêtés,
Les faibles mouvements, les dures fermetés :
Mais voulez-vous avoir plus claire connaissance

Que mon espoir se meurt et ne change point?
Il tournoie à l'entour du point de la constance
Comme le Ciel tournoie à l'entour de son point.

Do not be astonished if my mind, which goes

From subject to subject driven by so many impulses

Since it has been banished in Love's estrangements,

Even though agile, does not change its location.

However it appears, whatever it does,

It has been planted on such a good foundation

That it would never wish to undergo changes,

Were it not that fire could move its place of origin.

These two opposites are detained in me alone,

The weak impulse, the harsh decisions of mind:

But do you wish to have a clearer knowledge

That hope dies in me and yet does not change?

It turns about the point of constancy

As the sky turns about its pivot point.

Sponde is a part of his century and his age in his preoccupation with movement, which is reflected, for example, in the revival of Greek atomism, the curiosity about the motion of the stars and their determining influences. The metaphor of the changing, moving sky which turns upon its axis shows this interest. The problem Sponde finds within himself is based upon a similar situation: inconstancy, always moving away from the beloved; yet his love turns about the fixed point of his wish to love sincerely and constantly.

Sonnets d'amour

XIX

Je contemplais un jour le dormant de ce fleuve
Qui traîne lentement les ondes dans la mer,
Sans que les Aquilons le fassent écumer
Ni bondir, ravageur, sur les bords qu'il abreuve.

Et contemplant le cours de ces maux que j'épreuve,
Ce fleuve, dis-je alors, ne sait que c'est d'aimer;
Si quelque flamme eût pu ses glaces allumer,
Il trouverait l'amour ainsi que je le trouve;

S'il le sentait si bien, il aurait plus de flots.
L'Amour est de la peine et non point du repos,
Mais cette peine enfin est du repos suivie,

Si son esprit constant la défend du trépas:
Mais qui meurt en la peine il ne mérite pas
Que le repos jamais lui redonne la vie.

One day I contemplated the quiet flow of this river

Which slowly carries its waves into the sea,

Nor does the north wind cause it to froth

Or rage, ravaging, upon the shore it waters.

Contemplating the passage of misfortunes that I feel,

This river, I then said, does not know what it is to love.

If some flame might have set its ice on fire,

It would find love to be as it is for me.

If it felt so truly, the river's course would have more waves.

Love belongs not to quietude, but to pain,

Yet this pain is finally followed by repose

If love's constant awareness keeps the pain from death:

But he who dies in pain does not deserve

That repose should ever give him back his life again.

There is here a violent shift of viewpoint from the previous sonnets. Sponde has searched history, contemporary events and science for analogies to the argument that love continues and has permanency despite the threat of change and separation. In this sonnet we have violence again; we also have images of flowing movement (water, melting ice, river, waves). Existence is defined as co-existence of these two forces. So there is movement of the mind around the theme of the awareness of pain; there is also pain (the torments of love). The one keeps the other from disappearing.

Sonnets d'amour

XX

Les Toscans bataillaient, donnant droit dedans Rome,
Les armes à la main, la fureur sur le front,
Quand on voit un Horace avancer sur le pont
Et d'un coup arrêter tant d'hommes par un homme.

Après un long combat, ce brave qu'on renomme
Vaincu, non de valeur mais du grand nombre, rompt
De sa main le passage, et s'élance d'un bond
Dans le Tibre, se sauve, et sauve tout en somme.

Mon amour n'est pas moindre, et quoi qu'il soit surpris
De la foule d'ennuis qui troublent mes esprits,
Il fait ferme et se bat avec tant de constance

Que près des coups il est éloigné du danger;
Et s'il se doit enfin dans ses larmes plonger,
Le dernier désespoir sera son espérance.

The Tuscans battle, drive straight into the Roman city
With weapons in their hands, on their foreheads, fury,
Then one sees Horatio advance upon the bridge, and in one
Blow so many men are held back by one man.
After a long fight, this brave man whom we thought
Vanquished, not in valor but by the greater number,
Breaks his way through with his hand, jumps into the Tiber
In one leap, escapes, and thus saves all.
My love is not less than that, and although it may be overtaken
By a crowd of worries that trouble my wits,
It stands firm and combats with so much constancy
That though near misfortune it escapes danger.
And if it must at last plunge into tears,
The last despair will be its hopeful promise.

———

The iconography of the poem can be interpreted as a problem of multiplicity and singleness (which is eventually related to that of distance and nearness). Tuscans, weapons, the river, all suggest the *crowd of worries, fortune's blows, tears.* Against this multiplicity stands *one blow, one man, one leap, love,* firmness of attitude, the location of danger at one distant point. This quasi-mathematical outlook is Mannerist in that the equation is not squared: the return to multiplicity (*larmes*) becomes a kind of oneness (a single hope). The figure is broken, the emotional perspective, which should be in a line, turns out disjointed. The last two lines, however, indicate the wish to restore an emotional unity: from despair, disintegration, will spring hope (increase of love, continued growth of love).

Sonnets d'amour

XXI

Non, je ne cache point une flamme si belle,
Je veux, je veux avoir tout le monde à témoin,
Et ceux qui sont plus près, et ceux qui sont plus loin ;
Dites, est-il au monde un amant plus fidèle ?

Ces secrètes humeurs (qu'hypocrites j'appelle)
Blâment secrètement à l'oreille en un coin
La peine que je prends d'en prendre tant de soin,
Tandis que chacun d'eux ses propres sens recèle.

Ainsi nous différons, que leurs coeurs sont couverts
Et que le mien fait voir ses mouvements ouverts ;
Ils ont raison, leurs sens sont bien dignes de honte :

Mais je ne puis rougir d'aimer si dignement,
Et plus mon bel amour tous leurs amours surmonte :
Il me le faut encor aimer plus constamment.

No, I do not hide such a beautiful flame of love;

I want, I want the whole world to witness bear,

Both those who are nearest and those who are farthest.

Tell me, is there in all the world a more faithful lover?

These secret moods (which I call hypocrite)

Lay blame (when secretly told in a corner)

On the concern I have to take such care of love,

While each one of those who speak gives it his own inter-
  pretation.

Thus we differ—their hearts are hidden

And mine makes visible its motion:

They are right—their words identify my shame.

But I can not blush from loving so worthily,

And the more my fair love all their loves must overcome

Must I still love more constantly.

Sponde here proposes the antithesis of light and dark; he dis-
tinguishes between what is hidden and what is open. The antithesis can be explained on several levels. There is the moral, or
public, viewpoint: the poet is blamed for the moods of love
which he does not attempt to hide. There is also the private
viewpoint, in regard to himself: he must love faithfully in the
way that his fair love (light) overcomes the loves (dark) of
those who are critical of the possibility of constant love. Finally,
stylistically, the reader— in Sponde— is usually in the same
position towards the poem as the viewer towards the painting:
the light needs to be brought into the foreground for greater
effectiveness.

Sonnets d'amour

XXII

On dit que dans le ciel, les diverses images
Des astres l'un à l'autre ensemble rapportés
Engendrent ici bas tant de diversités
Et tantôt de profits et tantôt de dommages:

Tous les états leur font à leur tour leurs hommages,
L'un baisse, l'autre hausse: et tant de dignités
Ont en maintes façons certains points imités
Qui leur font et laisser et perdre leurs visages.

Mon amour sûr se trouve exempt de ces rigueurs,
Si ce n'est pour accroître encore ses vigueurs,
Mais non pas pour jamais d'un seul moment descendre.

Non pas s'il me fallait descendre dans la mort!
En somme il est (s'il faut par le ciel le comprendre)
Ferme ni plus ni moins que l'étoile du Nord.

They say that, in the sky, the various images

Of the stars as they approach one another

Engender here below as many differences

Of fortune, sometimes for good, sometimes for ill.

All conditions of men, in their turn, pay them homage:

One man's estate declines, the other's rises. These several

Dignities have, in many ways, in many places, limits

Which enable them, at once, to keep and lose their ranks.

My certain love is exempt from such change,

Unless it is to increase the more its strength,

But not ever, even for a single moment, to decrease.

Not even were it necessary for me to descend into death

Would my love depart. In short (if we go by heaven's charts),

It is neither more nor less steady than is the North Star.

Sponde here uses the device of an emblem from astrology, the North Star. Primarily this choice offers the reader a sense of perspective: the stars in relation to one another, a line of homage from man to stars, the rise and fall of fortune. The poet's love is exempt, except insofar as it gains strength from the struggle with adverse forces. The notion of perspective is then broken: diversity enters to be contrasted with the singleness of purpose of his love and his refusal to descend, (to sink downwards) towards death. The lesson of the heavenly perspective is clear: the influence of the North Star is direct, continuous; so is his love.

Sonnets d'amour

XXIII

Il est vrai, mon amour était sujet au change,
Avant que j'eusse appris d'aimer solidement,
Mais si je n'eusse vu cet astre consumant,
Je n'aurais point encor acquis cette louange.

Ores je vois combien c'est une humeur étrange
De vivre, mais mourir, parmi le changement,
Et que l'amour lui-même en gronde tellement
Qu'il est certain qu'enfin, quoiqu'il tarde, il s'en venge.

Si tu prends un chemin après tant de détours,
Un bord après l'orage, et puis reprends ton cours,
En l'orage, aux détours, s'il survient le naufrage

Ou l'erreur, on dira que tu l'as mérité.
Si l'amour n'est point feint, il aura le courage
De ne changer non plus que fait la vérité.

It is true my love was subject to deception
Before I had learned to love firmly and well.
But if I had not seen that star which consumes all
I would not have acquired love's commendation.
Now I see how strange a humor it is to live,
Only to die, amid this changing world, and that love
Itself complains so much of each change it is certain
That, at last, love—though slow—takes its revenge.
If you take a route after many detours,
Or a shore after a storm and then take up your way again—
In this storm, in these detours—then, if a shipwreck happens
Or a straying from the way, one will say to you, 'tis deserved.
Love will have the courage, if not feigned,
To change no more than truth is ever false.

Sponde here expounds what we may call a dialectic of love.
Like the traveler who, once having found the right way, will-
fully retraces the false, so love— if it seeks the wrong way
knowingly— will meet with disaster. But no penalty is at-
tached to following the false way through ignorance, since detours, misfortunes, unhappy turns, are the natural condition of
life. Faithfulness is observed, love is not punished for not taking
a right way. But lack of faith in the love relationship will be
punished by the death of that relationship.

Sonnets d'amour

XXIV

Mon Soleil, qui brillez de vos yeux dans mes yeux,
Et pour trop de clarté leur ôtez la lumière,
Je ne vois rien que vous, et mon âme est si fière
Qu'elle ne daigne plus aimer que dans les cieux.

Tout autre amour me semble un enfer furieux,
Plein d'horreur et de mort, dont m'enfuyant arrière
J'en laisse franchement plus franche la carrière
A ceux qui font plus mal et pensent faire mieux.

Le plaisir, volontiers, est de l'amour l'amorce,
Mais outre encor je sens quelque plus vive force
Qui me ferait aimer malgré moi ce Soleil:

Cette force est en vous dont la beauté puissante,
La beauté sans pareille, encor qu'elle s'absente,
Attire cet amant, cet amant sans pareil.

My Sun, whose rays shine from your eyes into my eyes,

And, for too much brightness, take from them their light,

I see only you, and my soul is so proud that in the skies

She does disdain all love's delight.

All other love seems to me hell's fury,

Full of horror and death, from which I flee

And behind, unhesitatingly, I leave the way there freer

For those who act worse in thinking they act better.

Pleasure, of course, is love's bait.

But, apart from that, I feel a livelier force

That would make me love this Sun whate'er I thought.

This force is in you whose beauty's power,

Beauty without parallel, even though absent,

Draws on this lover, this matchless lover.

Sponde addresses the beloved as the sun, a commonplace of
French and Italian sonneteers. But the implication of darkness
is again involved. Blindness occurs, and it becomes centered in
the source of light. This darkness he accepts. The other, the
dark hell of those who cannot appreciate true love, who accept
love only for pleasure (thereby obscuring the real purpose of
love), he rejects. This iight-darkness contrast is a force: as so
frequently for Sponde, he phrases the compulsion of love in
terms which make us think of mechanistic physics, a kind of
astral magnetism draws him—though, in a way, blind and un-
guided (the absent love)—towards the source of energy. There
is, morever, a Neo-Platonic tone of the *vertu* of love which leads
the lover to the dwelling place of light.

Sonnets d'amour

XXV

Contemplez hardiment tous ceux qui font coutume
De se sacrifier à l'autel des beautés,
Vous verrez que le vent de leurs légèretés
Leur éteint le brasier aussitôt qu'il l'allume.

Mais moi, qui si longtemps à vos yeux me consume,
Je ne consume point pourtant mes fermetés,
Et d'autant plus avant au feu vous me mettez,
Plus l'or de mon amour à durer s'accoutume.

Pour vous, belle, le tout de ce Tout ne m'est rien,
Ces biens sont pauvretés au regard de ce Bien,
Et vous servir tant plus que mille et mille empires.

S'en trouve qui voudra vivement offensé,
Pour moi j'aimerais mieux mourir en vos martyres,
Que vivre au pus grand heur qui puisse être pensé.

Contemplate boldly all those who make it a habit
To sacrifice themselves on the altar of beauty:
You will see that the wind of their frivolity
Puts out the flame as quickly as 'tis lit.
But I, who for so long waste away before your eyes,
I do not consume all my resolve.
And the more you place me in front of the fire,
The more my lover's gold learns to endure.
For you, my love, the all of this All is nothing for me.
This world's goods are poverty in the light of that Good,
And serving you worth so much more than a thousand
   thousand empires.
There are those whom these thoughts deeply wound.
For me I would rather die through the martyr's torture
   you inflict,
Than live in the greatest fortune that can be found.

———————

The key-word is *autel*—the altar on which takes place the sacrifice of love. There are, however, two kinds of altars: the one of
false gods, frivolity, inconstancy, the praise of the world; and
the other of true love, the constant flame, the true good. The
attitude is religious: the poet prefers to die, as a martyr, in the
service of this love than to renounce it in favor of the world's
fortune. We think of the use of the word *autel* in Racine, where
there is a similar dual implication; yet it is clear in Racine that
there is eventually no choice but resolution and catharsis through
passion, a choice not evident in Sponde. Again we have the dif-
ference between "Mannerist indecision," based on the restlessness
inherent in the concern over constancy and inconstancy, and
"Classical poise."

51

Sonnets d'amour

XXVI

Les vents grondaient en l'air, les plus sombres nuages
Nous dérobaient le jour pêle-mêle entassés,
Les abîmes d'enfer étaient au ciel poussés,
La mer s'enflait de monts, et le monde d'orages:

Quand je vis qu'un oiseau délaissant nos rivages
S'envole au beau milieu de ses flots courroucés,
Y pose de son nid les fétus ramassés
Et rapaise soudain ses écumeuses rages.

L'amour m'en fit autant, et comme un Alcyon,
L'autre jour se logea dedans ma passion
Et combla de bonheur mon âme infortunée.

Après le trouble, enfin, il me donna la paix:
Mais le calme de mer n'est qu'une fois l'année,
Et celui de mon âme y sera pour jamais.

The winds groaned in the air, darkest cloud

Upon darkest cloud was piled and hid the daylight from us,

The depths of Hell were lifted to the skies,

The sea with mountains, and the world with storms,
  was swelled:

Then I saw a bird, leaving our shore,

Fly to the very middle of these raging waves,

Place there the straws gathered from her nest

And suddenly calm the sea's frothy anger.

And so did love to me: like a Halcyon

It lodged the other day within my passion

And filled my unfortunate soul with fortune's good.

After the distress, at last, it gave me a quiet mind:

Yet the sea falls calm but once a year,

And the calmness of my soul will be there forever.

———

The sequence on love ends with the words *pour jamais*. This sonnet is, in its own way, a repetition of the whole exploration of Sponde's encounter with love, his rationalizations, the necessity to find an equilibrium matching the one existing in the physical universe. He acknowledges threats of storm, of war, of outrage. There is, however, a possibility which assuages this distress. As does the mythical bird Halcyon, that builds its nest once a year on the sea-waves and calms the stormy waters, so does his love pacify these threats. Love would then be the answer to the operation of time (change, chance, separation).

Sonnets de la Mort

I

Mortels, qui des mortels avez pris votre vie,
Vie qui meurt encor dans le tombeau du Corps,
Vous qui ramoncelez vos trésors, des trésors
De ceux dont par la mort la vie fut ravie:

Vous qui voyant de morts leur mort entresuivie,
N'avez point de maisons que les maisons des morts,
Ee ne sentez pourtant de la mort un remords,
D'où vient qu'au souvenir son souvenir s'oublie?

Est-ce que votre vie adorant ses douceurs
Déteste des pensers de la mort les horreurs,
Et ne sentez pourtant de la mort un remords,

Mortels, chacun accuse, et j'excuse le tort
Qu'on forge en votre oubli. Un oubli d'une mort
Vous montre un souvenir d'une éternelle vie.

Mortals, who from mortals are born and live

Life that dies again in the body's grave,

You who pile up your treasures, the wealth

Of those whose life was ravished by death:

You who see the death of the dead pursued,

Having no house but the house of the dead.

And yet, do you not feel in death some remorse,

From whence remembrance on remembering fades?

Is it that your life adoring its sweet pleasure

Fears the terrors of the thoughts from death's displeasure,

And might not envy the opposing envy?

Mortals, each one proves, and I excuse the wrong

Forged in your forgetting. Forgetting

Of a death shows remembering of life's eternity.

Sponde here offers several formulas concerning immortality. There is dissolution both material (*trésors, maison*) and intellectual (*souvenirs, oubli*), while the immortality of the soul is assured. We forget death, then remember its inevitability. The poet poses the question (in a kind of Mannerist obliqueness): is our life not able to contain such contrary notions? The answer would be an admonishment to reflect on these formulas; not to do so, would be in some way a wrong (*tort*).

Sonnets de la Mort

II

Mais si faut-il mourir! et la vie orgueilleuse,
Qui brave de la mort, sentira ses fureurs;
Les Soleils hâleront ces journalières fleurs,
Et le temps crèvera cette ampoule venteuse.

Ce beau flambeau qui lance une flamme fumeuse,
Sur le vert de la cire éteindra ses ardeurs;
L'huile de ce Tableau ternira ses couleurs,
Et ses flots se rompront à la rive écumeuse.

J'ai vu ces clairs éclairs passer devant mes yeux,
Et le tonnerre encor qui gronde dans les Cîeux.
Ou d'une ou d'autre part éclatera l'orage.

J'ai vu fondre la neige, et ces torrents tarir,
Ces lions rugissants, je les ai vus sans rage.
Vivez, hommes, vivez, mais si faut-il mourir.

Ah yes, one must die! and proud life which does speak
Disdainfully of death will feel its wrath and horror.
The suns shall burn these flowers in their daily fleeting splendor,
And time shall split open this wind-filled flask.
This fine torch which throws off flame and smoke
Upon the crude candle-wax shall put out its burning fires;
The paint of this picture shall cloud its colors,
And its waves will be broken upon the foaming bank.
I have seen these bright flashes of lightning pass before my eyes,
And the thunder too which grumbles in the heavens.
Either from one side or the other the storm will break.
I have seen the snow melt, these torrents become dry,
These roaring lions, I have seen them lose their fury.
Live, men, live, ah, yes! but surely one must die.

———

The poet cannot forget the intellectual solution to the problem of negation (*absence*). One thinks of Mallarmé, who too was dismayed when undirected action (here typified in Sponde's vocabulary by *brave, fureurs*) was pushed onto the stage. Destruction occurs (the flowers burnt, the smoke); the substance of life (*i.e.*, the oil of the painting as a composite function in the design) will tarnish; the river of life will break upon the shore. The sum total of the experience must be phrased in visual terms: *j'ai vu*, the flashes of lightning, the melting of the snows. The solution (as Mallarmé's answer to the *azur*) seems to accept what is feared, for Sponde the concept of death's embrace. Underlying this fear are the recurrent Renaissance themes of *carpe diem*, the concern for fleeting beauty, as well as a Stoic acceptance of death as a part of a great design or over-all reason for the annihilation of experience.

Sonnets de la Mort

III

Ha! que j'en vois bien peu songer à cette mort
Et si chacun la cherche aux dangers de la guerre!
Tantôt dessus la Mer, tantôt dessus la Terre,
Mais las! dans son oubli tout le monde s'endort.

De la Mer, on s'attend à resurgir au Port,
Sur la Terre, aux effrois dont l'ennemi s'atterre:
Bref, chacun pense à vivre, et ce vaisseau de verre
S'estime être un rocher bien solide et bien fort.

Je vois ces vermisseaux bâtir dedans leurs plaines
Les monts de leurs desseins, dont les cimes humaines
Semblent presque égaler leurs coeurs ambitieux.

Géants, où poussez-vous ces beaux amas de poudre?
Vous les amoncelez? Vous les verrez dissoudre:
Ils montent de la Terre? Ils tomberont des Cieux.

Ah! I see but few who think of their death
And, to be sure, each one looks for it in the dangers of war,
Sometimes upon the sea, sometimes upon the earth.
But, alas, everyone is off guard because he forgets death is
*   always near.*
At sea, one expects to come again into the port of grace;
On land, to vanquish fears that also fell the enemy.
In brief, each one intends to live, and this ship of glass
Is held to be a solid rock one cannot overturn.
I see these worms of men build upon the plain
The mountains of their designs, whose human summits
Seem almost to equal their ambitious hearts.
Giants, where do you cast up these fine heaps of dust?
You pile them up? You shall see them fall apart.
They climb from the earth? They shall fall from heaven's height.

Songer is here the important word. The poet has already come
to grips with paradox and with indeterminate action. He is now
engaged with imagination. He imagines the varying situations
when hope arises: a person drowning at sea reaches port. the
individual is spared from the horrors of war. Suddenly the perspective changes from the vastness of the sea and of battlefield
to the earth itself. The efforts of man's imaginative reason (ambition) crumble. They fall from the *cieux* they have attempted
to attain. Man overreaches himself. But the total effect is not a
moral statement concerning pride so much as a meditation upon
the intermediate stage when all constructive or irregular forms
(sleep, *cimes, amas*) have been dissolved. The moral reconstruc-
tion from imagination (as in the *Exercises* of St. Ignatius) has
not yet been possible.

Sonnets de la Mort

IV

Pour qui tant de trauvaux? pour vous? de qui l'haleine
Pantelle en la poitrine et traîne sa langueur?
Vos desseins sont bien loin du bout de leur vigueur
Et vous êtes bien près du bout de votre peine.

Je vous accorde encore une emprise certaine,
Qui de soi court du Temps l'incertaine rigueur;
Si perdrez-vous enfin ce fruit et ce labeur:
Le Mont est foudroyé plus souvent que la plaine.

Ces Sceptres enviés, ces Trésors débattus,
Champ superbe du camp de vos fières vertus,
Sont de l'avare mort le débat et l'envie.

Mais pourquoi ce souci? mais pourquoi cet effort?
Savez-vous bien que c'est le train de cette vie?
La fuite de la Vie, et la course à la Mort.

For whom so many travails? for yourself? whose breath
Beats in the breast and bears its languor out?
Your designs are far beyond the utmost of their strength,
And you are very near your trouble's final rest.
I grant you still a certain hold on life's span,
Which of itself flows—Time's uncertain rigor;
Ah, finally you are to lose this fruit and this labor:
The mountain is more often struck by thunder than the plain.
These envied scepters, these cast down treasures,
Haughty field of the camp of your proud virtues,
Are the dispute and the envy of avaricious death.
But why this care? but why this distress?
Can you really define this life's course?
The flight of life, the race towards death.

The theme of the poem is the *néant de la vie* discussed from the
points of view indicated by the breaks in the first two lines,
before the final extinction of life. Time allots a certain span for
activity (*vanitas vanitatum, fruit et labeur*). A definition of
tragedy is apparent in that fate (as equivalent to time) strikes
overambitious pride. But this fate is not Greek, not regular,
not a law governing man's relations with the Gods. It is irregular, uncertain, final only at the end. And the question initially
posed is that the *néant* is simply *le débat et l'envie* of death:
le débat in the sense of flight of life, *l'envie* as the race towards
death. Movement does not, at the last, stabilize itself from contradictory forces within itself, which is the Baroque solution.
Rather the idea of movement remains ambivalent: it is both
means, understanding the life process, and end, the total result
of action.

Sonnets de la Mort

V

Hélas! contez vos jours: les jours qui sont passés
Sont déjà morts pour vous, ceux qui viennent encore
Mourront tous sur le point de leur naissante Aurore,
Et moitié de la vie est moitié du décès.

Ces désirs orgueilleux pêle-mêle entassés,
Ce coeur outrecuidé que votre bras implore,
Cet indomptable bras que votre coeur adore,
La Mort les met en gêne, et leur fait le procès.

Mille flots, mille écueils, font tête à votre route,
Vous rompez à travers, mais à la fin, sans doute,
Vous serez le butin des écueils, et des flots,

Une heure vous attend, un moment vous épie,
Bourreaux dénaturés de votre propre vie,
Qui vit avec la peine, et meurt sans le repos.

Alas! count your days: the days which have gone
Are already dead for you, those which are yet to come
Shall all die at the moment of their newborn dawn.
And half of life is by half Death's kingdom.
These proud desires piled up pell-mell.
This furious heart that your heart adores:
Death tortures them and brings them all to trial.
A thousand waves, a thousand reefs, impede your way:
You break across, but at last, with no appeal or stay,
You will be the plunder of the reefs and the waves.
An hour waits for you, a moment spies
Upon you, unnatural executioners of your own lives,
Who live your days in travail, and die without repose.

The reader experiences here the intensity with which the idea of death overwhelms us. First, death goes with us throughout life, past and future. In contrast to this continuous presence is the human situation, without pattern (*pêle-mêle*); filled with the unforeseen (*mille écueils*); struggling with force (*le butin*), a force which is frequently against nature (*bourreaux dénaturés*) and nature's product (*notre propre vie*). In the unresolved tension which thus exists (*vit avec la peine, meurt sans le repos*) stands the executioner and judge, death. Intensity is thus achieved through the contrast of the uneven line of life and the direct line of death, which must exist together, yet in opposition.

Sonnets de la Mort

VI

Tout le monde se plaint de la cruelle envie
Que la nature porte aux longueurs de nos jours
Hommes, vous vous trompez, ils ne sont pas trop courts
Si vous vous mesurez au pied de votre vie.

Mais quoi? je n'entends point quelqu'un de vous qui dit:
Je me veux dépêtrer de ces fâcheux détours,
Il faut que je revole à ces plus beaux séjours,
Ou séjourne des Temps l'entresuite infinie.

Beaux séjours, loin de l'oeil, près de l'entendement,
Au prix de qui ce Temps ne monte qu'un moment,
Au prix de qui le jour est un ombrage sombre,

Vous êtes mon désir: et ce jour, et ce Temps,
Où le Monde s'aveugle et prend son passetemps,
Ne me seront jamais qu'un moment et qu'une Ombre.

All the world complains of the cruel envy
By which Nature would rob our days' disparity:
You of this world deceive yourselves, they go not too soon
If you measure yourselves by your lives' span.
What! I do not understand at all the man who would say:
I would like to escape this bothersome delay,
I must fly back to those more beautiful mansions
Where dwells time's infinite intentions.
O wonderful mansions, far from the eye, near to the under-
standing,
Compared to which, today is only a moment's measure,
Compared to which, day is a dark shadowing.
You are my desire: and this day and this time,
Wherein the world makes itself blind, and takes its pleasure,
Will never to me but a moment and a shadow limn.

The problem of time, which lies at the core of the *Sonnets de la Mort*, is especially evident in this poem. The stylistic device is a kind of circle, or rising spiral. For example, Sponde speaks first of physical aspects (*longueurs, courts, mésurés*) which are lifted to the area of infinite time (*l'entresuite*). Conviction of truth of Christian belief is described in a similar two-level manner: *loin de l'oeil, près de l'entendement* (in contrast to Pascal's *le coeur et la raison,* which stand on the same though opposite levels). Truth is, by definition, a kind of spatial paradox: time here and time there. *Désir* here is focalized in the distant *beaux séjours*. Life itself evolves in concentric ambiguities: darkness (in the verb *s'aveugle*) consists of the repetition of a single act of misunderstanding of Divine purpose. The noun *passetemps* suggests going from one action to another, yet takes on the substance of a figured *Ombre*.

Sonnets de la Mort

VII

Tandis que dedans l'air un autre air je respire,
Et qu'à l'envi du feu j'allume mon désir,
Que j'enfle contre l'eau les eaux de mon plaisir,
Et que me colle à Terre un importun martyre,

Cet air toujours m'anime, et le désir m'attire,
Je recherche à monceaux les plaisirs à choisir,
Mon martyre élevé me vient encor saisir,
Et de tous mes travaux le dernier est le pire.

A la fin je me trouve en un étrange émoi,
Car ces divers effets ne sont que contre moi:
C'est mourir que de vivre en cette peine extrême.

Voilà comme la vie à l'abandon s'épart:
Chaque part de ce Monde en emporte sa part,
Et la moindre à la fin est celle de nous-mêmes.

And while within the air another air I breathe,
And while, as does the fire, I light my desires,
And against the tide, I increase the tides of my pleasures,
And an importune martyrdom holds me to the earth,
This air always animates me, desire draws me on;
I seek the greatest span of pleasures I can choose.
Acute martyrdom comes then and seizes me again,
And of all my troubles the last is the most intense.
At the last I find myself in a strange anxiety,
These different states are not for, but against me.
To die, to live,— the same in this extremity.
This life dissolves, as though by unreason,
Each part of this world carries away its own portion:
And the least of these, at the end, we call our mortality.

This sonnet analyzes the four elements: air, fire, water, earth.
Each is the emblem, the pre-figuration of an emotional state: the
heavenly aspiration, love, the pomps of this fluctuating world,
suffering. The fusion of these diverse elements is impossible,
however frequently it is attempted. We are reminded of St.
Teresa's *muero porque no muero*, for only death can gather together the rending forces of these elements. Only death can resolve the anguish of the equation: what the body wishes, the
soul forbids; what the body does not wish, the soul desires. Life
is a haphazard dispersal (*à l'abandon*) whose integrating factor
is death. But still we have no idea of death as a moral function
in relation to right and wrong. We experience in the poem primarily the poet's sincerity in his anguish before the imminent
approach of death.

Sonnets de la Mort

VIII

Voulez-vous voir ce trait qui si raide s'élance
Dedans l'air qu'il poursuit au partir de la main?
Il monte, il monte, il perd: mais hélas! tout soudain
Il retombe, il retombe, et perd sa violence.

C'est le train de nos jours, c'est cette outrecuidance
Que ces Monstres de Terre allaitent de leur sein,
Qui baise ores des monts le sommet plus hautain,
Ores sur les rochers de ces vallons s'offense.

Voire, ce sont nos jours: quand tu seras monté
A ce point de hauteur, à ce point arrêté
Qui ne se peut forcer, il te faudra descendre.

Le trait est empenné, l'air qu'il va poursuivant
C'est le champ de l'orage: hé! commence d'apprendre
Que ta vie est de Plume, et le monde de Vent.

Do you see this dart which rises so directly
Into the air which it pursues when it leaves the hand?
It climbs, it climbs, it vanishes. But alas! quite suddenly
It falls again, falls, its vigor lost.
Thus is our days' course; it is this presumption
That these earthly monsters nurse in their breasts,
Those who touch now the highest peak of the mountain,
Now run against these valleys' rocky walls.
In truth, these are our days: when you have climbed
To this height, stopped at that turn
Which cannot be continued, you must descend.
The dart is feathered, the air where it continues to ascend
Belongs to the storm. Ah! begin to learn
Your life is like the arrow's feather, the world is like the wind.

This poem continues Sponde's effort to find a way out of the
ever present threat of dissolution, of the body, the reason, the
human personality, as they function in this life. The dart has
purpose (flight through the air) ; but this purpose once accom-
plished, by its accomplishment is destroyed, terminated. Thus
all action in life continually carries out a purpose (*allaitent, baise,
s'offense*), although the purpose once affected is consummated.
From general activity the emphasis is shifted to the specific *nos
jours*. We are at an impasse. Sponde must turn his viewpoint
around and go back to the metaphor of the dart. He indicates
that life is the dart, the world is the air through which the dart
moves. Although the eventual meaning is not stated, the implication seems to be a lesson of humility and the relative impor-
tance of man's reason in understanding any possible purpose to
existence.

Sonnets de la Mort

IX

Qui sont, qui sont ceux là, dont le coeur idolâtre
Se jette aux pieds du Monde, et flatte ses honneurs?
Et qui sont ces Valets, et qui sont ces Seigneurs?
Et ces âmes d'Ebène, et ces faces d'Albâtre?

Ces masques déguisés, dont la troupe folâtre
S'amuse à caresser je ne sais quels donneurs
De fumées de Court, et ces entrepreneurs
De vaincre encor le Ciel qu'ils ne peuvent combattre?

Qui sont ces louvoyeurs qui s'éloignent du Port?
Hommagers à la Vie, et félons à la Mort,
Dont l'étoile est leur Bien, le vent leur Fantaisie?

Je vogue en même mer, et craindrais de périr
Si ce n'est que je sais que cette même vie
N'est rien que le fanal qui me guide au mourir.

Who are they, those whose idolatrous heart
Is thrown at the feet of the world, adores the world's
Honors? And who are these servants, and who these lords?
And these souls of ebony, these features of alabaster?
These disguised masks, whose mad troupe
Is pleased to flatter anyone who hands out
The trifles of the court; those who attempt
To vanquish once more the Heaven that they can not overcome?
Who are these captains who tack about, stand off from port?
Those who, paying homage to life, betray death,
Whose star is their own good, the wind their fancy's notion?
I float on the same sea, and would fear to be lost
Were it not that I know this same life I span
Is nothing but the beacon that guides me to my death.

Sponde still seeks an answer to his question, where is the single unifying factor in the diversity of the world? He sees the hierarchy of social status, ambitions. Sponde uses the image of the sailor who refuses to be guided toward the haven by the true North Star and who faces, therefore, possible destruction at sea because of his arrogance and vanity. (Compare *Sonnets d'Amour*, xxiii). For the poet, on a similar sea of life, life itself becomes the reason for dying, a preparation for a "happy death." In one way we have a Renaissance art of dying, which has its roots in Stoic influences. But the suggestion of banality is relieved by the note of conviction in the combat of light and dark. Others have souls of ebony and faces of alabaster: Sponde has the white light of such discipline in life as guides him across the dark sea. There is no chiaroscuro, no reconciliation.

71

Sonnets de la Mort

X

Mais si mon faible corps (qui comme l'eau s'écoule
Et s'affermit encor plus longtemps qu'un plus fort)
S'avance à tous moments vers le seuil de la mort,
Et que mal dessus mal dans le tombeau me roule,

Pourquoi tiendrai-je raide à ce vent qui saboule
Le Sablon de mes jours d'un invincible effort?
Faut-il pas réveiller cette Âme qui s'endort,
De peur qu'avec le corps la Tempête la foule?

Laisse dormir ce corps, mon Âme, et quant à toi
Veille, veille et te tiens alerte à tout effroi,
Garde que ce Larron ne te trouve endormie:

Le point de sa venue est pour nous incertain,
Mais, mon Âme, il suffit que cet Auteur de Vie
Nous cache bien son temps, mais non pas son dessein.

But if my feeble body, which like the flowing water goes,

And endures longer than another's health,

This body advances every moment towards the threshold of
    death,

And misfortune upon misfortune rolls me into the grave's throes.

Why should I hold myself stiff against the wind which heaps

Together the sands of my days with an invincible effort?

Is it not necessary to awaken that soul which sleeps,

For fear that with the body the storm might trample it?

Let this body sleep, my soul, and as for you, keep

Your vigil and hold yourself alert to all fears and strife,

Be watchful that this thief does not find you in sleep.

The moment of his arrival is for us uncertain.

But, my soul, it is sufficient that the author of this life

Hides from us his time, but not at all his purpose.

Here Sponde speaks specifically of the body. Like a stream which rolls over the pebbles of the stream-bed toward the sea, so the existence of the human body goes inevitably towards death. The care of the soul moreover is watchfulness lest the body be taken by surprise and be unprepared for death. The image of waiting is taken from the parable of the thief in St. Matthew. The conclusion is clear: the moment of death is uncertain although its coming is sure. With the poet the reader has an equally acute sensation, that he, too, is waiting for the revelation of God's purpose to us.

Sonnets de la Mort

XI

Et quel bien de la Mort? où la vermine ronge
Tous ces nerfs, tous ces os; où l'Âme se départ
De cette orde charogne, et se tient à l'écart,
Et laisse un souvenir de nous comme d'un songe?

Ce corps, qui dans la vie en ses grandeurs se plonge,
Si soudain dans la mort étouffera sa part,
Et sera ce beau Nom, qui tant partout s'épart,
Borné de vanité, couronné de mensonge.

A quoi cette Âme, hélas! et ce corps désunis?
Du commerce du monde hors du monde bannis?
A quoi ces noeuds si beaux que le Trépas délie?

Pour vivre au Ciel il faut mourir plutôt ici:
Ce n'en est pas pourtant le sentier raccourci,
Mais quoi? nous n'avons plus ni d'Hénoch ni d'Êlie.

And what good to say of Death? where vermin gnaw

All these nerves, these bones, where the soul abandons

This horrid carrion, holding itself aside, leaves

Behind a memory of us that is like a dream?

This body, which in life plunges into its own ambition's need,

Suddenly in death will put out its life's portion,

Will be this noble Name, which is spread abroad,

Ringed in by vanity and crowned with lies.

For what purpose the soul, alas! and this body torn

Apart, banished, out of this world, from any commerce

With it? Why these fine knots that death unties?

In order to live in Heaven one must rather die on earth.

There is no question of a shortened path,

Alas! we have no longer here either Enoch or Elias.

This sonnet, too, defines the body's rôle, its purpose (*bien*) once the soul has left it. The visual impression of the body's death makes us think of Baudelaire's *La Charogne*, where the revolting sight before us becomes a *correspondance* of the necessity of death to complete and give meaning to life. Sponde states that we each must face this corruption and its inevitability; only Enoch and Elijah in the Old Testament, who were translated directly into Heaven, were spared this dissolution of the body. The divine purpose is clear and comforts our distress; in order to gain regeneration and integration into the divine plan, the body must die. The necessity of *si le grain ne meurt* is evident.

Sonnets de la Mort

XII

Tout s'enfle contre moi, tout m'assaut, tout me tente,
Et le Monde et la Chair, et l'Ange révolté,
Dont l'onde, dont l'effort, dont le charme inventé
Et m'abîme, Seigneur, et m'ébranle, et m'enchante.

Quelle nef, quel appui, quelle oreille dormante,
Sans péril, sans tomber, et sans être enchanté,
Me donras-tu? Ton Temple où vit ta Sainteté,
Ton invincible main, et ta voix si constante?

Et quoi? Mon Dieu, je sens combattre maintes fois
Encor avec ton Temple, et ta main, et ta voix,
Cet Ange révolté, cette Chair, et ce Monde.

Mais ton Temple pourtant, ta main, ta voix sera
La nef, l'appui, l'oreille, où ce charme perdra,
Où mourra cet effort, où se perdra cette onde.

Everything rises up against me, besieges me, tempts me,
The world and the flesh, and the angel in revolt;
The sea of fortune, the power of the flesh, the snare's delight,
Cast me down, Lord, shake me, and hold me prisoner.
What ship, what prop, what sleeping ear,
Without peril, without falling, without being cast into a spell,
Will you give me? Your temple, wherein dwell
Your holiness, your invincible hand, your so constant voice?
And then? My God, I feel that I struggle yet once
Again with your temple, and your hand, and your word,
This angel in revolt, this flesh, and this world.
Yet your temple, your hand, your voice will be
The ship, the prop, the ear, where this temptation will fail,
Where this power will die, and where this wave will be lost.

The final sonnet sums up those preceding; it has the form of
a triptych, each panel containing three parts: *s'enfle* (expansion),
m'assaut (from on high), *me tente* (outward). The "figura,"
the world, the flesh, the devil, stand in the middle. Then occurs
a restriction in the lower half: *m'abîme* (narrowness), *m'ébranle*
(shakedown), *m'enchante* (hold fast at one point). The idea
is carried throughout the whole poem: a ship which sails away
(movement), a support (something which holds a tottering
object), the sleeping ear (stilled motion). The Trinity is expressed in the Temple (the Father who is worshipped); the hand
(the Son, who carries out the Father's wishes); the voice (the
Spirit which speaks to men). The inversion at the end of the
first tercet relieves the repetition. Basically we have Sponde's
restless Mannerism, which strives for a firm and fixed resolution,
but which must ever give way to reversals, turnings, distress. But,
as is true with Baudelaire, the reader is convinced of a *"progression de foi,"* the culmination or resolution of this kind of movement. If the poems are not to be read as a complete statement of
such a *progression*, they can be read as a striving or struggling
towards such a belief.